LET'S TALK ABOUT

FAITH & FINANCE

FOR CHRISTIAN WOMEN

CREATING A GOD-CENTERED
APPROACH TO MANAGING MONEY

WWW.SMARTMONEYSISTERS.COM

ISBN: 9798332915994
Imprint: Independently Published

DEDICATION

To the women of faith who strive for financial freedom,

This book is dedicated to you, the resilient and courageous souls who are committed to transforming your financial lives with God's guidance. May you find the wisdom, strength, and inspiration within these pages to embrace new financial habits and make wise decisions that honor God.

To my family and friends who have supported me on this journey,

Thank you for your unwavering encouragement, love, and prayers. Your faith in me has been a source of strength and motivation.

To the Holy Spirit,

Thank you for being my constant guide and counselor. This book is a testament to your divine wisdom and unwavering support. May all who read it come to know your presence and experience the transformation that comes from partnering with you.

Be Blessed, Be Fruitful and Multiply!
Tesha D. Colston

CONTENTS

INTRODUCTION

Faith & Finance For Christian Women: Creating a God-Centered Approach to Managing Money is a culmination of some of the experiences I have had on my journey to breaking free from the control of money. Many of you may be able to relate to some of my experiences.

I wrote this book because I believe that God genuinely desires to transform our perspective on Him and money. My life experiences have taught me that God wants to be included in everything we care about, including our money. Most of us are not sure how to make God our financial partner partly because money has become a taboo subject in the church, but God wants to break that off of the church [you, the church] and teach us His ways concerning money.

This book is about exposing the lies and the misinformation that we have in our hearts concerning how we spend money. Understanding the truth and building healthy money habits will help us master this money thing for all of our days.

God gives us individual revelations, truths and strategies, but we must learn to come to Him not just our financial advisor(s) for financial wisdom and strategy. I pray that, by the time you have finished reading this book, you will fully understand how to seek God on a daily basis regarding your finances.

I believe that God wants to help us make good decisions concerning our money so that our way can be made prosperous.

"Keep this Book of the Law always on your lips; meditate on it day and night, so that you may be careful to do everything written in it. Then you will be prosperous and successful." (Joshua 1:8 NIV)

CHAPTER 1

THE SECRET TO BEING A GOOD STEWARD OF MONEY

"Wealth and honor come from you; you are the ruler of all things. In your hands are strength and power to exalt and give strength to all." (1 Chronicles 29:12 NIV)

Have you ever felt as though you'll never break free from the control of money? I used to feel the same way. I thought I would never overcome the cycle of not having enough and overspending. I constantly vowed to save a certain amount of money per paycheck or per month, hoping that by this time next year, I would have saved a specific amount or would have paid off certain bills. Yet, each year came and went without me reaching my goals. Sometimes, I had the willpower to save for a particular goal, but those habits never lasted, and I always found myself running out of money.

I wish I could tell you that "one day" the light bulb came on, I decreed and declared riches in my house and suddenly my life changed but that is not what happened.

What really happened is that "one day" the light bulb did come on and I had the realization that I needed to change the way I thought about how I steward money. Now, through daily work with the Holy Spirit, I live free from the control of money. This shift did not take place overnight. Spending time with the Holy Spirit is key to bringing you closer to God and that is what brings a lasting change in your financial habits.

If you find yourself where I once was, feeling like a financial breakthrough is out of reach, I'm here to tell you that with God, you can achieve it. God is powerful and capable of anything, and with Him, you can do all things. Will it happen overnight? Probably not. However, if you continue to seek God's help, you will start to see a shift in your financial situation.

This book is all about seeking God's help to achieve a true transformation in your financial life. The key is that God waits for you to come to Him so He can assist you. He wants to be involved in every aspect of our lives, including our financial well-being. God is the secret, so let's tap into His wisdom and guidance as we navigate this financial journey together.

To help you begin this life-changing process, I encourage you to practice spending dedicated time with God.

Here is a simple yet powerful activity to get you started:

- Set your timer for fifteen minutes and dedicate this time to sit with God and hear Him concerning your finances.
- You can play soaking music if you like.
- As you begin, start with a prayer to let God know you are here to talk about renewing your mind around money and its stewardship and that you want to know his thoughts on the matter.
- Listen to Him, for His still small voice.
- As you do that, meditate on key scriptures, and thank and praise Him.
- In the journal space provided, write His responses as He speaks to you, and note your main takeaways from this time with God.

Daily Affirmation

Ready? Repeat after me!

I am a faithful steward of God's resources, managing my money wisely and honoring Him in all my financial decisions.

Daily Prayer

Ready? Repeat after me!

God, teach me to be a good steward of the resources You have entrusted to me. Guide my financial decisions and help me to manage my money in a way that honors You.

In Jesus name, Amen.

CHAPTER 2

SETTING FINANCIAL BOUNDARIES

"Do not conform to the pattern of this world, but be transformed by the renewing of your mind. Then you will be able to test and approve what God's will is — his good, pleasing and perfect will." (Romans 12:2 NIV)

When you attend a financial class, you often come with the mindset of sacrifice. You brace yourself to make commitments that might make you and your household suffer.

However, in this book, you will find that it is easier to not commit to a spending plan. That's right, not commit! Contrary to popular advice, this book is not a quick and easy approach to the stewardship of money.

The plain truth is, if you want to be a good lifelong steward of the money you have been blessed to receive, you will need to renew your mind, spend with purpose, pay off your current debt, save and invest money, and give from your heart. This is not just for this season but for your entire life. As Thomas Edison said, "Opportunity is missed by most people because it is dressed in overalls and looks like work."

There is a misconception in the church that God does not require us to restrict things because we are under grace. However, God is not a "do whatever you want" God. He expects us to trust Him and to show our love for Him by being willing to give up all of what we want to Him, especially if they get in the way of us loving and trusting Him.

We have limits in other areas of our lives, so why is it so challenging to have limits with money? When we drive, it would be nice to go as fast as we want. However, on the highways, in school zones, and on city streets, there are speed limits. Are these limits bad? No, they keep us and others from harm. The same is true about how we spend money; there are consequences to spending however we want. Some of you may be experiencing those consequences right now. However, with the Holy Spirit's help, there can be a turnaround.

There are several ways to set limits with money, which we will call spending plans. There are different methods to establish a plan for your money. Let's briefly review four ways to start, and with the Holy Spirit's help, you can choose the one that is right for you.

1. 50/30/20 Plan

The 50/30/20 Plan is a balanced and straightforward approach to managing your finances. Here's how it works:

- **50% for Living Expenses:** This includes all your essential needs such as housing, utilities, groceries, transportation, insurance, and other mandatory bills. The goal is to ensure that half of your income is dedicated to maintaining a stable and secure lifestyle.

- **30% for Lifestyle Expenses:** This portion is for your personal enjoyment and discretionary spending. It covers dining out, entertainment, hobbies, vacations, and other non-essential items that enhance your quality of life.

- **20% for Savings:** This includes saving for emergencies, retirement, and other financial goals. It's crucial to prioritize this part to build a solid financial foundation and ensure future security.

2. Spend 1st Plan

The Spend 1st Plan is a more flexible approach where spending comes first, and savings are made from what remains. Here's how it works:

- **Plan Your Spending:** After receiving your income, you first plan how you will spend it on various expenses, both essential and discretionary.

- **Save Whatever is Left:** Once your spending plan is in place, the remaining funds are allocated to savings. This method requires discipline to ensure that savings are still a priority and not neglected.

3. Save 1st Plan

The Save 1st Plan emphasizes saving before spending. Here's how it works:

- **Pay Yourself First:** As soon as you receive your income, a predetermined percentage or amount is immediately set aside for savings. This ensures that saving is a non-negotiable part of your financial routine.

- **Spend the Rest:** The remaining funds are then allocated to living and lifestyle expenses. This plan prioritizes long-term financial health by making savings the top priority.

4. Fixed Plan

The Fixed Plan involves detailed budgeting with specific

categories. Here's how it works:

- **Allocate Earnings to Specific Categories:** Each month you divide your income into fixed categories such as housing, utilities, groceries, entertainment, savings, and debt repayment. Each category has a set limit that you adhere to strictly.
- **No Money Left Unplanned:** The goal is to ensure that every dollar has a purpose and is allocated to a specific category until there is no money left unaccounted for. This method helps in maintaining control over your finances and avoiding unnecessary spending.

Choosing the Right Plan

Spend some time in prayer and reflection, asking the Holy Spirit to guide you in choosing the spending plan that best suits your financial situation and goals. Remember, the key is to find a plan that you can commit to and that aligns with your values and priorities.

In the following pages you will see visual examples of each type of spending plan as well as journal pages to journal your conversation with God.

Visit our website to download budgeting sheets or visit us on Amazon to purchase budgeting books.

50/30/20 Budgeting Plan Example

Savings Donations 20%

Living Expenses 50%

Lifestyle Expenses 30%

Living Expenses 50%	Lifestyle Expenses 30%	Savings Donations 20%
Rent Mortgage	Personal Care	Tithes
Utilities	Hobbies	Emergency Savings
Gas	Travel	Donations
Electric	Internet/Cable	Purpose Savings
Water/Sewer	Dining Out	Debt Reduction
Garbage	Netflix, Amazon	Payments
Cell Phone	Prime	Investments
Groceries	Gifts	Retirement Savings
Household	Clothing	
Items	Fun Money	
Car Payments		
Car Insurance		
Gas		
Maintenance		
Minimum Debt Payments		
Student Loans		

SPEND 1ST MONTHLY BUDGET

Example

Income Sources

Take-home Pay	$
Addt'l Income	$
Total Income	$

Your Expenses	Amount
Housing	$
Transportation	$
Utilities	$
Subscriptions	$
Food	$
Medical	$
Dining, Entertainment, Travel	$
Other	$
Debt Payments	$
Household Items	$
Tithes	$
Donations	$
Total Expenses	$

Your Bottom Line

Total Income	$
Total Expenses -	$
Savings =	$

SAVE 1ST MONTHLY BUDGET

Example

Income Sources

Take-home Pay	$
Addt'l Income	$
Total Income	$

Your Bottom Line

Total Income		$
20% Savings	-	$
Left for Expenses	=	$

Your Expenses	Amount
Housing	$
Transportation	$
Utilities	$
Subscriptions	$
Food	$
Medical	$
Dining, Entertainment, Travel	$
Other	$
Debt Payments	$
Household Items	$
Tithes	$
Donations	$
Total Expenses	$

FIXED MONTHLY BUDGET

Example

	Category	Expected	Actual	Difference	Notes
Income	Income				
	Income				
Home Expenses	Mortgage/Rent				
	Electric/Gas				
	Water/Sewer				
	Garbage				
	Internet/Cable				
	Repairs				
Insurance	Health				
	Renters/Homeowners				
	Life				
	Auto				
Cars	Car Payments				
	Gas				
Living Expenses	Groceries				
	Dining Out				
	Household				
	Phone				
	Clothes				
	Personal Care				
Other	Entertainment				
	Charity/Gifts				
	Travel				
	Savings				
Debt	Credit Cards				
	Loans				
	Loans				
Totals	Total Income				
	Total Expenses				

Daily Affirmation

Ready? Repeat after me!

I set healthy financial boundaries
and honor them. These boundaries
protect my finances and lead me
to stability and peace.

Daily Prayer

Ready? Repeat after me!

God, give me the wisdom to set and maintain healthy financial boundaries. Help me to see them as a source of protection and guidance. Strengthen my self-control to honor these boundaries and walk in financial stability.

In Jesus name, Amen.

CHAPTER 3

PLANNED PROCRASTINATION

"No discipline seems pleasant at the time, but painful. Later on, however, it produces a harvest of righteousness and peace for those who have been trained by it."
(Hebrews 12:11 NIV)

Every time I said, "I will start my spending plan next paycheck," it never happened. Costco was my best friend and still is. Each paycheck, I would go food shopping there, armed with a list of only the necessary items. However, upon entering, I would be tempted by all the shiny objects, from household items to food. Before I knew it, I was far from my spending plan and in overspending mode. I would justify my purchases by saying, "Oh, it's just a small thing," or "We really need this," or "I forgot to put it on the list." Most of the time, those were just excuses. The truth is, if it wasn't on the list, we most likely didn't need it. Can you relate to my story?

I believe many of you have had similar experiences. Whether it's at the grocery store, during a stroll through the mall, or while browsing online, you can probably identify with purchasing items that were not in the plan.

Most often, I would enter the store with the intention of sticking to my spending plan. But before I knew it, I would find countless reasons to justify unplanned purchases, telling myself, "I will start my spending plan next paycheck."

Why do we do that? Why do we procrastinate on carrying out the spending plan? Is it because we never really wanted to follow the plan in the first place, or is it because procrastination allows us to spend without guilt, telling ourselves we will start it on the next paycheck?

When I was truly ready for this cycle to stop, I worked with the Holy Spirit to start the spending plan now, not later. I realized I needed His help to adhere to the plan, as I couldn't do it on my own. If we want to break free from the control of money, we will need to develop two key mindsets: working with the Holy Spirit in our spending and consistently following the plan.

Spend time with God asking the questions below. Look to the Holy Spirit for answers. As you seek, He will answer with the truth.

Take this time to reflect deeply, and allow the Holy Spirit to guide you towards the truth and the steps you need to take.

In what ways have I been a financial procrastinator?

What are the lies I have told myself for procrastinating in creating financial boundaries or not sticking to the spending plan?

Holy Spirit, what is the truth?

God, how would my life transform if I made the commitment to this lifelong spending plan?

What would I have to sacrifice to make this spending plan commitment?

God, how can I partner with You in this area?

Daily Affirmation

Ready? Repeat after me!

I take action on my financial goals today. I am proactive and diligent, breaking free from the cycle of procrastination.

Daily Prayer

Ready? Repeat after me!

God, help me to break free from procrastination. Give me the motivation and diligence to take action on my financial goals today. Guide my steps and keep me focused on the path You have set before me.

In Jesus name, Amen.

CHAPTER 4

BUT I LOVE TO SPEND MONEY

"Then he said to them, "Watch out! Be on your guard against all kinds of greed; life does not consist in an abundance of possessions." (Luke 12:15 NIV)

It was the first day of my vacation, and I had already gone off my spending plan! Not because I absolutely had to buy something, but because I didn't make enough effort to avoid the purchase. Special occasions are precisely when I need to stay on plan the most. I have to follow the plan, always, because I LOVE to spend money. Yes, it's true, I love to shop. I shop in person, online, over the phone, and in various ways, from business ideas to supporting my favorite food shops.

Over the years, I've also learned that I spend money not just because I love to but for emotional reasons. I love to spend money when I am happy, and I love to spend money when I need a pick-me-up. I have realized that I must make and follow a spending plan to manage this habit effectively.

Setting financial boundaries and limits, and sticking to them, is not a widely popular belief system.

However, we need limits, boundaries, and plans to help us say NO, that is not in the plan, or that is out of bounds.

What kind of person needs to set limits and stick to them? The type of person that:

- Loves to spend money or shop.
- Turns to shopping and spending money to fulfill emotional needs.
- Sees spending money as fun.
- Does not include God in the shopping and spending process.

That should just about cover everyone. I know it covers me. If I have my way, I will shop till I drop and mess up all the money. So, I have learned that I must have boundaries.

You've heard of the term shop-a-holic? Let's say that a shop-a-holic is a person who cannot stop shopping. Have you watched any of those hoarder shows? Is that you? It was me, and because of that, I started to avoid going out for fear of spending money. But God did not give us a spirit of fear, and He wants to help us break free from the control of money.

Spend time with God today answering the following questions.

Ask the Holy Spirit for truth, remembering that He is going to help transform your life in the area of finances.

Take this time to reflect deeply, and allow the Holy Spirit to guide you towards the truth and the steps you need to take.

Describe the life of a shop-a-holic? If that is you, what is your life like?

Are you the type of person that can shop and stay within the boundaries? Why or why not?

What would your life look like if you partnered with Holy Spirit in this area?

Daily Affirmation

Ready? Repeat after me!

I recognize and control my emotional spending. My financial decisions are guided by wisdom and purpose, not by fleeting emotions.

Daily Prayer

Ready? Repeat after me!

God, help me to overcome emotional spending. Teach me to recognize the triggers and to respond with wisdom and purpose. Guide my heart and mind so that my financial decisions honor You and reflect good stewardship.

In Jesus name, Amen.

CHAPTER 5

WHO LIKES BOUNDARIES?

"But godliness with contentment is great gain. For we brought nothing into this world, and it is certain we can carry nothing out. And having food and raiment let us be therewith content.." (1 Timothy 6:6-8 KJV)

One day I was in the store with my 3-year-old son. He wanted a bag of chips. I told him no, I wasn't going to purchase the chips today. He started crying, reaching for the bag of chips, and I told him no again. He started crying and just had a tantrum in the middle of the store. He acted like a true 3-year-old. He wanted what he wanted, and he wanted it now! Sometimes, I am much like that. I want what I want, and I don't want to wait — I want it now. Have you ever felt this way?

I believe at one point in our lives or another, we have all felt this way. We live in a world where rules often seem unnecessary. A world that says, "Go with your heart, do what you want, be who you want to be, and spend what you want to spend."

If we want to truly change our financial picture, we need to embrace a Kingdom mindset. When we do that, we understand that boundaries, limits, rules, and discipline are not bad — they are actually good for us.

Proverbs 29:18 KJV says, *"Where there is no vision, the people perish: but he that keepeth the law, happy is he."* The writer here is letting us know that where there is no plan, there will be consequences. The same applies to money. There are consequences to not making financial plans and following them.

If we want to manage our finances in a way that enables us to be effective for God, we need to set financial boundaries and follow them.

Reflective Questions

To help you internalize these concepts and apply them to your own life, spend time with God today reflecting on the following questions. Seek His guidance as you consider your financial boundaries and habits.

Allow the Holy Spirit to guide your thoughts and responses, leading you towards a more disciplined and godly approach to managing your finances.

Read Romans 3:31

Does this passage say that because we have faith we can do or buy what we want? If not, ask Holy Spirit what is it saying?

Read Romans 7:7

How can this scripture help us better understand why it's good to set financial boundaries?

Why would God want us to make and follow financial boundaries?

What will happen if we just buy what we want, whenever we want?

Daily Affirmation

Ready? Repeat after me!

I am content with what I have, trusting that God provides for all my needs. My contentment leads to peace and wise financial choices.

Daily Prayer

Ready? Repeat after me!

God, help me to cultivate a mindset of contentment. Help me to trust that You provide for all my needs. Let my contentment bring peace to my heart and guide me to make wise financial choices.

In Jesus name, Amen.

CHAPTER 6

DAY ONE OR ONE DAY

"Multitudes, multitudes in the valley of decision! For the day of the LORD is near in the valley of decision." (Joel 3:14 NIV)

Today is a day of decision on financial boundaries. If you haven't already, will you set financial boundaries today? We all know that what is easy to do is also easy not to do. It's always easier to say, "I will do that tomorrow." It can be difficult to commit to doing it today. I know I have had a lot of "tomorrow" experiences in my life. The question is, how do I get to the point where I make a commitment for today and not someday? That today will be my day one and not another "one day." I know that it is a sacrifice, and that a lifelong sacrifice is a bit scary. However, the blessing that is on the horizon for you will far outweigh that scary feeling.

I know that we don't take the first step of commitment for different reasons. If you are like me, you simply enjoy spending money. You don't like to limit yourself financially.

If this is your "why," take a moment and write what your life would look like if you set financial boundaries.

What would it be like without financial boundaries?

Then write down which one you like better and why.

Another reason we don't want to set financial boundaries is FOMO — the "fear of missing out." We live in a time where the messages we hear everywhere are, "Let me make you an offer you can't refuse," or "You must get this before the sale expires," and who knows if it's coming back again. God forbid we miss out on that low, low offer or fast action bonus.

If we have financial boundaries, we would need to face the fact that there are things we will not be able to do or buy on a whim or as they present themselves. We may miss the sale at the mall or the grocery store. We may not be able to purchase that course or take that class, etc., because we have a spending plan.

Let's take a moment and dig into this. Write all of the benefits and the cons of keeping your financial options open in the columns below.

Most of the time, it's clear how much the sacrifice is truly worth.

Benefits

Cons

Here is a big struggle of mine: I don't like rules, and when I hear them, I want to break them or question why we even have them. I look for another way. Maybe, at times, I have that spirit of entitlement that says, "I deserve this." If you are like me, then you will need to revisit the pros and cons often as a reminder of the advantages of creating and sticking to your spending plan.

The last thing I want to talk about is the fear of being seen as a failure. Somehow, sacrificing through spending plans, financial plans, or budgeting makes us feel like we have failed in money management. However, that is a lie, and that is not how others see it.

Most people understand that having and maintaining a spending plan is positive and often wish they would do it themselves. It actually gives you authority in the area of finances. It shows that you are stable, capable, disciplined, and that you steward your life well.

What are some other lies you have been told about spending plans that have created fear? What is the truth? Write the lies and the truths in the boxes below.

And you shall know the truth, and the truth shall make you free!

Lies

Truths

If you have decided to commit to developing financial boundaries and a plan, here are three ways to start:

1. **Give It A Try Plan** - Example: Set one financial boundary because, how do you eat an elephant? One bite at a time. This could be writing out all of your expenses and committing to a month of not buying one thing that will chip away at your money.

2. **Go A Little Deeper Plan** - Example: Make a commitment to no unnecessary spending.

3. **Go All-In Plan** - Example: Set up your spending plan using one of the strategies in Day Two and commit to no unnecessary spending.

Writing down your commitment is a powerful step toward achieving your financial goals. It solidifies your intentions and serves as a constant reminder of your dedication. By specifying when you will start and detailing what you are committing to, you create a clear path for yourself to follow. This written commitment will help you stay accountable and focused on your journey to financial freedom.

I will commit to following plan: _____

My plan start date: _____

Here are the habits that I am committed to following in order to make this successful:

(Write down your success habits here)

Daily Affirmation

Ready? Repeat after me!

I am committed to developing good financial habits that honor God and lead to financial freedom.

Daily Prayer

Ready? Repeat after me!

God, help me to develop and maintain good financial habits. Guide my actions and decisions so that they reflect Your wisdom and lead to financial freedom. Strengthen my resolve to honor You with my finances.

In Jesus name, Amen.

CHAPTER 7

LEARNING TO BE CONTENT

"Whoever loves money never has enough; whoever loves wealth is never satisfied with their income. This too is meaningless." (Ecclesiastes 5:10 NIV)

I've always had this dream in my head of walking down the California boulevard with Saks 5th Avenue and Tiffany bags in my hands, screaming "shop till you drop." Taking a shopping break at a local coffee shop, and as I sit, I'm thinking about which store to visit next. I must have red bottoms! I tell myself, "I need another pair of red bottom shoes."

However, the reality is that this is not reality. If I were to actually live like that, what would my financial picture be? It would more likely involve being stressed out from being broke, possibly taking those packages back after the consequences of my splurge day set in.

Why do we feel the need to have all that stuff anyway? Where did we get the idea that we need more than what we already have?

Is it the billboards we see as we drive the highways, the commercials we see between our favorite TV shows that get louder to make sure we hear them? Could it be the TV shows themselves, the magazines we read, or the neighbor next door? Where are these messages coming from?

In conversations with people who have visited or lived in other nations, I often hear that they don't have those lies to compete with. No matter where we picked it up, it's all a lie. The truth is these things will never satisfy us, and we will always find ourselves wanting more until we learn to be content with what we have and where we are in life.

Take some time to write down your thoughts and reflections on the following questions. Consider how embracing contentment and setting financial boundaries can transform your life. By doing so, you can align your financial habits with your faith and experience greater peace and stability.

Reflect on these insights and let them guide you in making lasting changes to your financial habits.

Read Philippians 4:10-13. What do you think Paul meant in this passage of scripture, and how can you apply it to your finances?

What do you think are the natural consequences of always indulging yourself?

Ask Holy Spirit what are the spiritual consequences of always indulging yourself?

Think about the times when you have overdone it. Was your life better or not, and why or why not?

Daily Affirmation

Ready? Repeat after me!

I understand the importance of my financial habits and am committed to aligning them with God's principles.

Daily Prayer

Ready? Repeat after me!

God, reveal to me the true nature of my financial habits. Help me to align them with Your principles and to seek Your guidance in all my financial decisions. Transform my heart and mind to reflect Your wisdom.

In Jesus name, Amen.

CHAPTER 8

THE HEART OF FINANCIAL HABITS

"The heart is deceitful above all things, and desperately wicked: who can know it?" (Jeremiah 17:9 KJV)

The more I worked on building good financial habits, the more I realized the truth of the scriptures. I understood how deceitful my thoughts were and how much I need to, and will continue to, ask God to create in me a clean heart. I rarely just come right out and say, "I am going to go off my spending plan," or "I'm going to break the bank today." No, my mind says things like, "I really don't spend that much money," but when I look back over my bank statements, my expenses prove that was a lie.

Here are some other lies we tell ourselves:

- "I'm following my plan" - when really, we follow it only when we are in between paychecks and money is tight.
- "I really need that" - when realistically, we could have done without "that," whatever "that" is.
- "I've been following the plan so closely I deserve this" - when we haven't reached any of our financial goals.

Reflective Questions

- What are some of the lies your mind has told you?
- What is the truth?

Write them out in the columns below.

Lies   Truths

Have you ever wondered why we lie to ourselves? Why don't we ever just tell ourselves the real deal? We lie to ourselves because we know what we should not be doing, so we find ways to make it okay. We look for ways to legitimize our reasons for breaking our commitment.

I don't want you to walk away thinking you can never spend money your way. There are times when you forget about an occasion or an unexpected emergency comes up and you need to step over your financial boundaries. Those situations are few and far in-between and most often can be planned for and put into your monthly spending plans.

Reflection Activity

- Think about times when you have told yourself these lies to convince yourself it was okay to step over your financial boundaries. Why do you think you didn't tell yourself the truth of the matter?

What do you think would happen if you told yourself the truth?

Scripture Reading and Reflection

Read James 1:5-8, 22. What does it say about how you can break free from justifying poor actions? What does it say you can do to break free?

Ask the Holy Spirit what you can do to break free from justifying poor financial habits.

Spend some time reflecting on these questions and scriptures, asking the Holy Spirit for guidance and truth. By facing the lies we tell ourselves and embracing the truth, we can make better financial decisions and honor God with our stewardship.

Daily Affirmation

Ready? Repeat after me!

I understand the deeper motivations behind my financial habits and am committed to aligning them with God's principles.

Daily Prayer

Ready? Repeat after me!

God, reveal to me the deeper motivations behind my financial habits. Help me to align my actions and decisions with Your principles. Transform my heart and guide me to develop habits that honor You and lead to financial stability and peace.

In Jesus name, Amen.

CHAPTER 9

I DESERVE TO SPLURGE

"Those who want to get rich fall into temptation and a trap and into many foolish and harmful desires that plunge people into ruin and destruction." (1 Timothy 6:9 NIV)

Do you ever feel like when payday comes, you deserve to splurge? I do! It can be challenging not to feel that way because our world culture says that you deserve to have a good life — after all, YOLO (you only live once).

These messages encourage us to spend money in different ways. We feel that we have a right to spend money whenever we want and on whatever we want. We also feel like we have the right to live the life we have always wanted to live. I am a big proponent of living an abundant life. What these messages don't tell you is that when you establish good financial habits, you can achieve those goals.

I don't know about you, but here is my challenge: I don't want to go through the process. I want it to all work right now. So, when I am faithful to my spending plan for a pay period or two but don't see a change in my financial picture, I get discouraged. When that happens, I go to the store and make a purchase that is outside of my spending plan. I mean, how much more can I really suffer? But this thinking perpetuates the situation and slows my progress. Then what ends up happening is I stop altogether, tearing up the spending plan.

When that happens, you will need to be transformed by the renewing of your mind.

Reflective Activity

Think about your financial expectations, spending habits, and future goals, and ask yourself the following questions:

- Spending money should be:
- I should not have to:
- I should be able to:
- It's not fair that:

Ask the Holy Spirit for His truth about each of these statements.

Spend time reflecting on these questions and seeking the Holy Spirit's guidance to transform your mindset and establish better financial habits.

By renewing your mind and aligning your financial decisions with God's wisdom, you can break free from the cycle of impulsive spending and move towards achieving your financial goals.

Daily Affirmation

Ready? Repeat after me!

I resist the urge to splurge and make mindful financial decisions that align with my long-term goals.

Daily Prayer

Ready? Repeat after me!

God, help me to resist the desire to splurge and to make mindful financial decisions. Strengthen my self-control and remind me of my long-term goals. Guide me to use my resources wisely and honorably.

In Jesus name, Amen.

CHAPTER 10

THINK ABOUT WHAT YOU'RE THINKING ABOUT

"Finally, brothers and sisters, whatever is true, whatever is noble, whatever is right, whatever is pure, whatever is lovely, whatever is admirable — if anything is excellent or praiseworthy — think about such things."

(Philippians 4:8 NIV)

There were times along this journey when I thought, "I'll never be able to do this. I'll never be able to have good financial habits. I'll never be able to control my spending. I'm just too lazy to do this budget thing," and the list of lies I would tell myself just went on. However, as I continued, I learned that those were lies. I realized that I had to keep going on this financial journey and, as I go, recognize those lies, find the truths, and meditate on the truths.

John 8:31-32 says, *"Then said Jesus to those Jews which believed on Him, If ye continue in my word, then are ye my disciples indeed; And ye shall know the truth, and the truth shall make you free."*

If you are in any way like me, you may have felt or still feel the same way, hopeless at times. These lies come either when you have not achieved victory in a specific financial area, when you are about to break your spending plan, or after you have already broken it. But the truth is that your financial fight is different than it was before. You are opposing the lies with the truth! It is the truth that is setting you financially free.

To truly have victory in your finances, you will need to stay in the fight. It's a journey, not a sprint, and you did not obtain poor financial habits overnight.

It would be nice if we could just have all the money we wanted and spend however we want. For most of us, that won't happen. Even if it did, habits are habits, good or bad. How we are with little is how we are with much. How we do one thing is how we do everything, so we have to develop the habits that foster a disciplined mind.

We can only do that with God's help. Here's the kicker… God wants to help us. God wants us to be actively involved in the renewing of our money mindset and He wants to be a part of our transformation. We must remember that God is key to our transformation.

the same way, hopeless at times. These lies come either when you have not achieved victory in a specific financial area, when you are about to break your spending plan, or after you have already broken it. But the truth is that your financial fight is different than it was before. You are opposing the lies with the truth! It is the truth that is setting you financially free.

To truly have victory in your finances, you will need to stay in the fight. It's a journey, not a sprint, and you did not obtain poor financial habits overnight.

It would be nice if we could just have all the money we wanted and spend however we want. For most of us, that won't happen. Even if it did, habits are habits, good or bad. How we are with little is how we are with much. How we do one thing is how we do everything, so we have to develop the habits that foster a disciplined mind.

We can only do that with God's help. Here's the kicker... God wants to help us. God wants us to be actively involved in the renewing of our money mindset and He wants to be a part of our transformation. We must remember that God is key to our transformation.

Reflective Activity
Think about times when you have spent without thought of

responsibility. As you do, reflect on the following questions:

What were the lies that came to mind?

Did you seek God in your decision or after? Why or why not?

What do you think would happen if you talked to God in these situations?

Ask the Holy Spirit, what is the truth of these lies?

How will your money mindset change if you thought about the lies you are hearing and then asked the Holy Spirit for the truth of the lies each and every time?

Spend time reflecting on these questions and seeking the Holy Spirit's guidance to transform your mindset. By recognizing the lies and replacing them with God's truth, you can develop better financial habits and experience true financial freedom.

Daily Affirmation

Ready? Repeat after me!

I recognize the lies I have believed about money and replace them with God's truth. I am committed to wise financial stewardship.

Daily Prayer

Ready? Repeat after me!

God, I ask for Your truth to fill my mind and heart. Help me to see through the lies and embrace Your wisdom. Guide me in making decisions that honor You and bring me closer to financial freedom.

In Jesus name, Amen.

CHAPTER 11

IS OVER SPENDING A SIN?

"There is treasure to be desired and oil in the dwelling of the wise; but a foolish man spendeth it up." (Proverbs 21:20 KJV)

I am one who has tended to ask the question, "Is this a sin or not?" in some areas of my life. What I've found is that this is another way my mind tries to justify what I've done or what I want to do.

Sometimes, it seems as though it's my last-ditch effort to win the internal battle over good vs. bad behaviors. Who do you know from the Bible that did this same thing? I think of Adam and Eve and the serpent.

The serpent presented to Eve the fruit from the tree of the knowledge of good and evil. His presentation went something like this: "Did God really say, 'You must not eat from any tree in the garden'?"

That's what we do as well. Did God really say not to do this or that? Did God really say not to buy what I want? Did God really say I need to establish or maintain a spending plan?

Is this really a sin? I won't get into the doctrine of whether this is a sin or not, but the Bible does say, *"If anyone, then, knows the good they ought to do and doesn't do it, it is sin for them." (James 4:17 NIV)*

However, what I think is important is why we do what we do or do not do. Knowing if it's a sin or not does not change behaviors most of the time, at least not change that stands the constant temptations of today's culture. I must come to the realization that I must change. To change my financial picture, I must first deal with why I do what I do. It brings me to ask this question: are you turning to spending to cope with life?

One of the things I love about God is that He will use our circumstances to draw us closer to Him. His ultimate goal is for us to get back to His original design, in His image and likeness.

God gave us the gift of choice, even though He knows that sometimes we will choose the very things that are, in the end, not to our benefit.

Like Adam and Eve, they had a choice. There were consequences to their choices. If they had continued to not eat from that tree, what would their life have been like? The same goes for us. When we choose to have and maintain financial boundaries, what is or what would our life be like?

Reflective Activity

Think about a time when you've chosen to go against what you knew was the right thing to do and write the situation below.

- How did it end up for you and others that were affected by your decision?
- Why do you think you made that choice?
- What is the potential outcome of making a better choice?

I wonder what our world would be like if Adam or Eve had said to that serpent, "Let me check with God," before they made that decision. Likewise, what would your life be like if you checked with God before you made a purchasing decision?

- What would your life be like if you invited the Holy Spirit to join you when you go to the grocery store, when you go to the mall, or even when you shop online?
- How would your life change if you invited God into your financial decisions?

Practical Steps to Involve God in Financial Decisions

1. Pray Before Shopping: Take a moment to pray and ask for wisdom and guidance before making any purchase.
2. Consult the Bible: Reflect on relevant scriptures that emphasize stewardship, contentment, and wisdom.
3. Set Clear Boundaries: Establish and maintain spending plans that align with godly principles.
4. Seek Accountability: Share your financial goals and struggles with a trusted friend or mentor who can offer support and prayer.
5. Reflect and Meditate: Regularly meditate on God's Word to reinforce a mindset of stewardship and gratitude.

By inviting God into your financial decisions and seeking His guidance, you can develop better financial habits and experience a more abundant and fulfilling life.

Daily Affirmation

Ready? Repeat after me!

I avoid the trap of overspending and seek to use my finances in a way that pleases God.

Daily Prayer

Ready? Repeat after me!

God, help me to avoid the trap of overspending. Teach me to use my finances in a way that pleases You. Guide my decisions and help me to be a faithful steward of the resources You have given me.

In Jesus name, Amen.

CHAPTER 12

BEGIN WITH THE END IN MIND

"Suppose one of you wants to build a tower. Won't you first sit down and estimate the cost to see if you have enough money to complete it?" (Luke 14:28 NIV)

When I started on this financial freedom journey, I found that one of the reasons I did not take my financial journey seriously was that I did not have a big picture view of my life. I didn't have any goals and I really didn't have my very own whys. I didn't really know why I needed to or wanted to change my financial picture. I had to deconstruct my thinking.

I learned that having a good understanding of my own fundamentals was another key to creating and sticking to a financial plan. I knew the answers to the questions, but with God, I was able to know what I truly wanted and why. God knows how to pull it out of you, and He wants to help you.

Take time to sit with the Holy Spirit and ask Him to help you as you reflect on the following questions:

Reflective Questions

- What does my financial picture look like now?
- How do I feel about my current financial picture? Why?
- What do I want my financial picture to look like?
- How would I feel about this financial picture? Why?
- What do I want to achieve? Short-Term Goals
- What do I want to achieve? Long-Term Goals
- How do I plan to achieve my goals?

As you take time to thoughtfully answer these questions. Here are some steps to guide you in this process:

- Prayer and Reflection: Begin by praying and asking the Holy Spirit to guide your thoughts and reflections. Seek His wisdom and clarity as you answer each question.
- Honest Assessment: Be honest with yourself about your current financial situation. Reflect on your feelings about it and why you feel that way.
- Vision for the Future: Envision what you want your financial picture to look like. Think about the emotions and reasons behind this vision.
- Set Goals: Define your short-term and long-term financial goals. Be specific about what you want to achieve.

- Action Plan: Create a plan outlining the steps you need to take to achieve your goals. Consider practical actions and strategies that align with godly principles.
- Regular Review: Make it a habit to regularly review your goals and progress. Adjust your plan as needed and continue to seek God's guidance.

Take some time to write down your thoughts and answers to the reflective questions. The following pages provide a structured way to do it.

By taking the time to reflect and plan with the Holy Spirit's guidance, you can build a strong foundation for your financial journey and achieve lasting financial freedom.

What does my financial picture look like now?
(Write your detailed assessment here)

Asset Sources		Income Sources	
Asset Name	Value	Income Source	Amount
——————	——————	——————	——————
——————	——————	——————	——————
——————	——————	——————	——————
——————	——————	——————	——————
——————	——————	——————	——————
——————	——————	——————	——————
——————	——————	——————	——————
Total	——————	Total	——————

Debt		Liabilities	
Debt Name	Amount	Liability Name	Amount
——————	——————	——————	——————
——————	——————	——————	——————
——————	——————	——————	——————
——————	——————	——————	——————
——————	——————	——————	——————
——————	——————	——————	——————
——————	——————	——————	——————
Total	——————	Total	——————

How do I feel about my current financial picture? Why?

What do I want my financial picture to look like?

Asset Sources		Income Sources	
Asset Name	Value	Income Source	Amount
___	___	___	___
___	___	___	___
___	___	___	___
___	___	___	___
___	___	___	___
___	___	___	___
___	___	___	___
Total	___	Total	___

Debt		Liabilities	
Debt Name	Amount	Liability Name	Amount
___	___	___	___
___	___	___	___
___	___	___	___
___	___	___	___
___	___	___	___
___	___	___	___
Total	___	Total	___

How would I feel about this financial picture? Why?

What do I want to achieve?

Short Term Goals

What do I want to achieve?

Long Term Goals

How do I plan to achieve my goals?

Daily Affirmation

Ready? Repeat after me!

I begin with the end in mind, setting clear financial goals and working diligently to achieve them.

Daily Prayer

Ready? Repeat after me!

God, help me to begin with the end in mind. Grant me clarity in setting my financial goals and the diligence to achieve them. Guide my steps and keep me focused on the vision You have given me.

In Jesus name, Amen.

CHAPTER 13

BUT EVERYONE ELSE IS BUYING IT

"We do not dare to classify or compare ourselves with some who commend themselves. When they measure themselves by themselves and compare themselves with themselves, they are not wise." (2 Corinthians 10:12 NIV)

Don't you hate it when it seems like everyone you are associated with spends their money how they want to spend it? When you are heading for a change, it seems like everyone is going in the opposite direction. All of your circle is going to the mall shopping or buying courses online; Amazon packages are coming to their doors. It's just not fair! After all, shouldn't life be fair? If you think your life is not fair, just keep living and you'll find out how much of a lie that is.

Who could blame us for thinking this way? Every message in our culture lends itself to the need for our lives to measure up to others, and if it's not, then it's not fair. What is the truth of that lie? The truth, most likely, is if you were to rate your life on a scale of 1-10, you would be coming very close to a 10! Have you checked out other nations, other cities in our nation, other people in our nation, not just our circle or the ones we see on TV? If we are to measure our lives against all the lives, we would probably change it to be rated a 10!

Have you considered what decisions they made, what sacrifices they have had in order to make the purchases you see them making? I have found that not everything that glitters is gold. I have seen people who appear to have it all struggle financially. I have seen people who make a lot of money struggle in their management of money.

I read a web article on BusinessInsider.com that said, "Researchers from the San Francisco Federal Reserve found that people who earn 10 percent less than their neighbors are 4.5 percent more likely to commit suicide." The measuring ourselves by ourselves thing is some serious business!

So, I want to encourage you today, not to look to the left or to the right, but to keep YOUR why and YOUR vision in front of you as your purpose for achieving financial freedom.

Creating Your Personal Vision Statement

A personal vision statement helps you keep your values in mind, guiding you to make good financial decisions and develop good money habits. It is a picture of your future self, incorporating all the important components of your life and career in one statement. It tells who you want to be, what you want to do, how you want to feel, what you want to own, and who you want to associate with.

Although your personal vision helps you to see into the future, it must be based in the present tense. It is a statement of who you are and who you are becoming. It is the blueprint for the process of creating your life. Your vision is where you are headed.

Reflective Exercise

1. Visualize Your Future Self: Close your eyes and see your future self. Visualize the person you are. Can you see what you are doing? Do you see who you are with? Take note of what you have accomplished. Identify what is important to you. Now, open your eyes and write down what you saw.
2. Analyze Your Current Life: Now, analyze your life as it is but through the eyes of your future self. Do you see the changes you need to make to honor this vision and lead a powerful life? Write down the changes.
3. Craft Your Personal Vision Statement: Take a moment to craft your personal vision statement. Invite the Holy Spirit to help you.

Sample Personal Vision Statement Structure

- Who You Are: Describe your character, values, and personal qualities.
- What You Do: Outline your career or life activities and how they align with your purpose.
- How You Feel: Express the emotions and states of being you aspire to maintain.
- What You Own: Mention the possessions or assets that are important to you.
- Who You Associate With: Identify the types of relationships and communities you want to be part of.

Example Personal Vision Statement

"I am a faithful steward of God's resources, living a life of integrity, generosity, and financial wisdom. I actively pursue my career with purpose and passion, making a positive impact on those around me. I feel content and fulfilled, enjoying peace and abundance in all areas of my life. I own a comfortable home, free of debt, and invest wisely for the future. I am surrounded by loving family and supportive friends who encourage and uplift me. My life reflects God's grace and provision, and I use my blessings to bless others."

Take the time to carefully craft your own personal vision statement. Let it serve as your guiding star, helping you make decisions that align with your values and goals, leading you towards a fulfilling and financially free life.

My Vision Statement

Daily Affirmation

Ready? Repeat after me!

I have a clear personal vision for my financial future, and I am committed to achieving it with God's guidance.

Daily Prayer

Ready? Repeat after me!

God, help me to build a clear personal vision for my financial future. Guide me in setting and achieving my goals. Strengthen my commitment to align my financial decisions with Your will.

In Jesus name, Amen.

CHAPTER 14

LIFE IS A JOURNEY NOT A SPRINT

"Trust in the Lord with all your heart and lean not on your own understanding; in all your ways submit to him, and he will make your paths straight." (Proverbs 3:5-6 NIV)

I thought I had mastered this financial habit thing, but moving and then starting a business proved that was a lie — in my Maury Povich voice!

When I moved from Seattle to North Carolina, I bought things that were not in the budget. I went on trips that I probably should not have until I reached one of my major financial goals. I made investments that turned out to be scams, not investments, and spent money I did not need to spend on the relocation. When I started my financial coaching business, I did it again! I started buying things for my business-like coaching packages because a coach needs a coach!

What I found was that there are levels to this. This financial freedom road is a journey, not a sprint. You don't just get there, but with the help of the Holy Spirit, you will get there. We've talked about uncovering lies and discovering truths.

As thoughts come that are not from God, you can nip them in the bud. You have authority over what comes through your mind. Not everything that comes to your mind is from you or God. You have the power and the authority over your mind and what stays in it. Those thoughts might include some of the ones we've talked about before, like "I'll never be able to manage my finances God's way."

When thoughts come that you know are not godly, you can ask God, "What is this that is coming against me?" Listen to what He says is coming against you.

Spiritual Activity

Take some time to reflect and place in the blanks what is coming against you. Then, declare the following:

- I nail _____ to the cross. I break all agreements I've made with _____ known or unknown.
- God, I repent for joining with _____.
- God, I ask you to send _____ away from me.
- God, what do you want to give me in place of _____? Journal what God says.

Practical Application

I learned from the study "God Owns It All" by Ron Blue that "every financial decision is a spiritual decision." So, it's no wonder that ungodly thoughts would come our way. We have the power and the spiritual weapons to dismantle all the works of darkness.

- Recognize the Lies: Identify the ungodly thoughts and lies that come to your mind regarding your finances.
- Ask for God's Truth: Pray and ask God to reveal the truth and to show you what is coming against you.
- Declare and Repent: Declare the ungodly thoughts nailed to the cross, break agreements with them, and repent for joining with them.
- Seek God's Replacement: Ask God what He wants to give you in place of those lies and ungodly thoughts.

Closing Reflection

Reflect on how you can trust in God's guidance and lean not on your own understanding. Acknowledge Him in all your financial decisions, and He will direct your paths.

By continually seeking God's guidance and replacing lies with His truth, you will grow stronger in managing your finances according to His will.

Remember, this journey is about progress, not perfection, and with the help of the Holy Spirit, you will achieve financial freedom.

Daily Affirmation

Ready? Repeat after me!

I trust God in every financial season, knowing that He is my provider and sustainer.

Daily Prayer

Ready? Repeat after me!

God, I trust You in every financial season. You are my provider and sustainer. Bring peace and stability to my finances as I place my faith in You. Guide me through each season with Your wisdom and grace.

In Jesus name, Amen.

CHAPTER 15

INVITING GOD INTO OUR MONEY DECISIONS

"Take delight in the Lord, and he will give you the desires of your heart. Commit your way to the Lord; trust in him and he will do this: He will make your righteous reward shine like the dawn, your vindication like the noonday sun."

(Psalm 37:4-6 NIV)

This book was primarily focused on our relationship with God and financial decisions. Many people do not realize that God wants to be part of every financial decision we make, and when we include Him, we will have good success. Partnering with God will help us to establish new financial habits and apply financial wisdom to our lives.

We know that when we start to change our ways, sometimes discouragement will come. We may want to think about the road ahead and how much further we have to go to reach our financial goals. But we have a counselor who is here to help us remember to be thankful for all that we have and how far we have already come in our financial journey. He is here to help push us to completely change how we think about money and how we use it.

God uses His time with us and His word to change our attitudes and bring us to a place where we yield our dollars and cents to Him.

Sis, we have so much to be thankful for. Instead of focusing on what we don't have or should not buy, let us keep our minds focused on the goodness of God and all that He has done for us. Let us focus on Kingdom goals and what God wants us to accomplish here on earth. Let us focus on the next generation and the legacy we are leaving them. Let us use our finances to help us build a deeper relationship with God.

Thankfulness will actually help us to break cycles of financial defeat and push us past barriers that wrong thinking may have built up in our lives.

Reflective Activity

Let's begin to ask God for what we want and thank Him for everything that He has already done in our lives.
The scripture says: *"Be careful for nothing; but in everything by prayer and supplication with thanksgiving let your requests be made known unto God." - Philippians 4:6*

Why do you think it is so powerful to pray with thanksgiving?

As you continue your efforts to break free from the chains of money, remember to pray with thanksgiving, inviting the Holy Spirit into every money decision you make. God is waiting for your invitation of His power to be fully active in your finances, and He will transform your financial picture.

Personal Commitment

I pray that you will continue to work with the Holy Spirit in all of your financial decisions, that you will continue to renew your financial mind as you spend time with Him.

As a result of reading this book, journal the following:

- What will you do now to continue to renew your financial mind and habits?
- What steps will you take to include God in every financial decision?
- How will you practice thankfulness in your financial journey?
- What specific goals will you set to ensure you are aligning your financial decisions with God's will?

Take some time to write down your commitments and actions to continue growing in financial wisdom and stewardship.

By consistently inviting God into your financial decisions and practicing thankfulness, you will experience a profound transformation in how you manage and view your finances. Trust in Him, and He will guide you to financial freedom and abundance.

Daily Affirmation

Ready? Repeat after me!

I am committed to continual growth and learning in my financial journey, seeking God's wisdom every step of the way.

Daily Prayer

Ready? Repeat after me!

God, I commit to continual growth and learning in my financial journey. Guide me, teach me, and help me to keep improving. May Your wisdom lead me to achieve my goals and honor You with my finances.

In Jesus name, Amen.

12 -Month Financial Goal Planner

As you continue your efforts I have included this 12 month financial goal planner. This goal planner is your guide to the achievement of your financial goals. Remember to seek God as you set your goals and strategies. Ask Him questions to really uncover what is in your heart and his plans for this season. Get the truth of your daily actions and resolve to a comitted life of maintaining good financial habits.

Month of:

SUN	MON	TUES	WED	THU	FRI	SAT

Important Dates

_____ _____
_____ _____
_____ _____
_____ _____
_____ _____
_____ _____
_____ _____
_____ _____

My Financial Goal

⚑ WHAT IS MY FINANCIAL GOAL?

💡 WHY DO I WANT TO ACHIEVE THIS GOAL?

❓ HOW WILL I ACHIEVE MY GOAL?

⌲ WHAT TOOLS WILL I USE TO ACCOMPLISH MY GOAL?

My Financial Strategies

⚑ MY FINANCIAL GOAL IS ....

_____

_____

💡 STRATEGY #1

📋 5 ACTION STEPS

#1 _____
#2 _____
#3 _____
#4 _____
#5 _____

💡 STRATEGY #2

📋 5 ACTION STEPS

#1 _____
#2 _____
#3 _____
#4 _____
#5 _____

💡 STRATEGY #3

📋 5 ACTION STEPS

#1 _____
#2 _____
#3 _____
#4 _____
#5 _____

Reflection

 DID I ACCOMPLISH MY FINANCIAL GOAL?

WHAT HAVE I LEARNED IN THE PAST 21 DAYS?

_____
_____
_____
_____

WHAT NEW SKILLS HAVE I ACQUIRED?

_____
_____
_____
_____
_____

WHAT WERE THE BIGGEST CHALLENGES I HAD TO OVERCOME?

_____
_____
_____
_____
_____

WHAT ARE MY NEXT STEPS?

_____
_____
_____
_____
_____

Month of:

SUN	MON	TUES	WED	THU	FRI	SAT

Important Dates

My Financial Goal

🚩 WHAT IS MY FINANCIAL GOAL?

⬜ WHY DO I WANT TO ACHIEVE THIS GOAL?

❓ HOW WILL I ACHIEVE MY GOAL?

✈ WHAT TOOLS WILL I USE TO ACCOMPLISH MY GOAL?

My Financial Strategies

🚩 MY FINANCIAL GOAL IS ....

_____

_____

💡 STRATEGY #1		📋 5 ACTION STEPS
		#1 _____
		#2 _____
		#3 _____
		#4 _____
		#5 _____

💡 STRATEGY #2		📋 5 ACTION STEPS
		#1 _____
		#2 _____
		#3 _____
		#4 _____
		#5 _____

💡 STRATEGY #3		📋 5 ACTION STEPS
		#1 _____
		#2 _____
		#3 _____
		#4 _____
		#5 _____

Reflection

🚩 DID I ACCOMPLISH MY FINANCIAL GOAL?

✅   ❌

⚙️ WHAT HAVE I LEARNED IN THE PAST 21 DAYS?

_____

_____

_____

_____

🪄 WHAT NEW SKILLS HAVE I ACQUIRED?

_____

_____

_____

_____

_____

WHAT WERE THE BIGGEST CHALLENGES I HAD TO OVERCOME?

_____

_____

_____

_____

🏃 WHAT ARE MY NEXT STEPS?

_____

_____

_____

_____

_____

Month of:

SUN	MON	TUES	WED	THU	FRI	SAT

Important Dates

_____	_____
_____	_____
_____	_____
_____	_____
_____	_____
_____	_____
_____	_____
_____	_____
_____	_____

My Financial Goal

WHAT IS MY FINANCIAL GOAL?

WHY DO I WANT TO ACHIEVE THIS GOAL?

HOW WILL I ACHIEVE MY GOAL?

WHAT TOOLS WILL I USE TO ACCOMPLISH MY GOAL?

My Financial Strategies

🚩 MY FINANCIAL GOAL IS ....

_____

_____

💡 STRATEGY #1

📋 5 ACTION STEPS

#1 _____
#2 _____
#3 _____
#4 _____
#5 _____

💡 STRATEGY #2

📋 5 ACTION STEPS

#1 _____
#2 _____
#3 _____
#4 _____
#5 _____

💡 STRATEGY #3

📋 5 ACTION STEPS

#1 _____
#2 _____
#3 _____
#4 _____
#5 _____

Reflection

 DID I ACCOMPLISH MY FINANCIAL GOAL?

WHAT HAVE I LEARNED IN THE PAST 21 DAYS?

_____
_____
_____
_____

WHAT NEW SKILLS HAVE I ACQUIRED?

_____
_____
_____
_____
_____

WHAT WERE THE BIGGEST CHALLENGES I HAD TO OVERCOME?

_____
_____
_____
_____
_____

WHAT ARE MY NEXT STEPS?

_____
_____
_____
_____
_____

Month of:

SUN	MON	TUES	WED	THU	FRI	SAT

Important Dates

My Financial Goal

WHAT IS MY FINANCIAL GOAL?

WHY DO I WANT TO ACHIEVE THIS GOAL?

HOW WILL I ACHIEVE MY GOAL?

WHAT TOOLS WILL I USE TO ACCOMPLISH MY GOAL?

My Financial Strategies

🚩 MY FINANCIAL GOAL IS ....

_____
_____

💡 STRATEGY #1	📋 5 ACTION STEPS
	#1
	#2
	#3
	#4
	#5

💡 STRATEGY #2	📋 5 ACTION STEPS
	#1
	#2
	#3
	#4
	#5

💡 STRATEGY #3	📋 5 ACTION STEPS
	#1
	#2
	#3
	#4
	#5

Reflection

⚑ DID I ACCOMPLISH MY FINANCIAL GOAL?

⚙ WHAT HAVE I LEARNED IN THE PAST 21 DAYS?

_____
_____
_____
_____

✦ WHAT NEW SKILLS HAVE I ACQUIRED?

_____
_____
_____
_____
_____

WHAT WERE THE BIGGEST CHALLENGES I HAD TO OVERCOME?

_____
_____
_____
_____

WHAT ARE MY NEXT STEPS?

_____
_____
_____
_____

Month of:

SUN	MON	TUES	WED	THU	FRI	SAT

Important Dates

_____   _____
_____   _____
_____   _____
_____   _____
_____   _____
_____   _____
_____   _____
_____   _____
_____   _____

My Financial Goal

⚑ WHAT IS MY FINANCIAL GOAL?

💡 WHY DO I WANT TO ACHIEVE THIS GOAL?

❓ HOW WILL I ACHIEVE MY GOAL?

✈ WHAT TOOLS WILL I USE TO ACCOMPLISH MY GOAL?

My Financial Strategies

🚩 MY FINANCIAL GOAL IS ....

_____

_____

💡 STRATEGY #1	📋 5 ACTION STEPS
	#1 _____
	#2 _____
	#3 _____
	#4 _____
	#5 _____

💡 STRATEGY #2	📋 5 ACTION STEPS
	#1 _____
	#2 _____
	#3 _____
	#4 _____
	#5 _____

💡 STRATEGY #3	📋 5 ACTION STEPS
	#1 _____
	#2 _____
	#3 _____
	#4 _____
	#5 _____

Reflection

🚩 DID I ACCOMPLISH MY FINANCIAL GOAL?

⚙️ WHAT HAVE I LEARNED IN THE PAST 21 DAYS?

_____

_____

_____

_____

_____

🪄 WHAT NEW SKILLS HAVE I ACQUIRED?

_____

_____

_____

_____

_____

🏔️ WHAT WERE THE BIGGEST CHALLENGES I HAD TO OVERCOME?

_____

_____

_____

_____

_____

🏃 WHAT ARE MY NEXT STEPS?

_____

_____

_____

_____

_____

Month of:

SUN	MON	TUES	WED	THU	FRI	SAT

Important Dates

_____   _____
_____   _____
_____   _____
_____   _____
_____   _____
_____   _____
_____   _____
_____   _____
_____   _____
_____   _____

My Financial Goal

WHAT IS MY FINANCIAL GOAL?

WHY DO I WANT TO ACHIEVE THIS GOAL?

HOW WILL I ACHIEVE MY GOAL?

WHAT TOOLS WILL I USE TO ACCOMPLISH MY GOAL?

My Financial Strategies

🚩 MY FINANCIAL GOAL IS ....

_____

_____

_____

💡 STRATEGY #1	📋 5 ACTION STEPS
	#1 _____
	#2 _____
	#3 _____
	#4 _____
	#5 _____

💡 STRATEGY #2	📋 5 ACTION STEPS
	#1 _____
	#2 _____
	#3 _____
	#4 _____
	#5 _____

💡 STRATEGY #3	📋 5 ACTION STEPS
	#1 _____
	#2 _____
	#3 _____
	#4 _____
	#5 _____

Reflection

 DID I ACCOMPLISH MY FINANCIAL GOAL?

✔ ✖

⚙ WHAT HAVE I LEARNED IN THE PAST 21 DAYS?

_____

_____

_____

_____

🪄 WHAT NEW SKILLS HAVE I ACQUIRED?

_____

_____

_____

_____

WHAT WERE THE BIGGEST CHALLENGES I HAD TO OVERCOME?

_____

_____

_____

_____

🏃 WHAT ARE MY NEXT STEPS?

_____

_____

_____

_____

Month of:						
SUN	**MON**	**TUES**	**WED**	**THU**	**FRI**	**SAT**

Important Dates

_____   _____
_____   _____
_____   _____
_____   _____
_____   _____
_____   _____
_____   _____
_____   _____
_____   _____

My Financial Goal

⚑ WHAT IS MY FINANCIAL GOAL?

💡 WHY DO I WANT TO ACHIEVE THIS GOAL?

❓ HOW WILL I ACHIEVE MY GOAL?

✈ WHAT TOOLS WILL I USE TO ACCOMPLISH MY GOAL?

My Financial Strategies

🚩 MY FINANCIAL GOAL IS ....

_____

_____

💡 STRATEGY #1	📋 5 ACTION STEPS
	#1 _____
	#2 _____
	#3 _____
	#4 _____
	#5 _____

💡 STRATEGY #2	📋 5 ACTION STEPS
	#1 _____
	#2 _____
	#3 _____
	#4 _____
	#5 _____

💡 STRATEGY #3	📋 5 ACTION STEPS
	#1 _____
	#2 _____
	#3 _____
	#4 _____
	#5 _____

Reflection

 DID I ACCOMPLISH MY FINANCIAL GOAL?

WHAT HAVE I LEARNED IN THE PAST 21 DAYS?

_____
_____
_____
_____

WHAT NEW SKILLS HAVE I ACQUIRED?

_____
_____
_____
_____
_____

WHAT WERE THE BIGGEST CHALLENGES I HAD TO OVERCOME?

_____
_____
_____
_____

WHAT ARE MY NEXT STEPS?

_____
_____
_____
_____
_____

Month of:

SUN	MON	TUES	WED	THU	FRI	SAT

Important Dates

_____   _____
_____   _____
_____   _____
_____   _____
_____   _____
_____   _____
_____   _____
_____   _____
_____   _____

My Financial Goal

⚑ WHAT IS MY FINANCIAL GOAL?

🔦 WHY DO I WANT TO ACHIEVE THIS GOAL?

❓ HOW WILL I ACHIEVE MY GOAL?

✈ WHAT TOOLS WILL I USE TO ACCOMPLISH MY GOAL?

My Financial Strategies

🚩 MY FINANCIAL GOAL IS ....

_____

_____

💡 STRATEGY #1

📋 5 ACTION STEPS

#1 _____
#2 _____
#3 _____
#4 _____
#5 _____

💡 STRATEGY #2

📋 5 ACTION STEPS

#1 _____
#2 _____
#3 _____
#4 _____
#5 _____

💡 STRATEGY #3

📋 5 ACTION STEPS

#1 _____
#2 _____
#3 _____
#4 _____
#5 _____

Reflection

🚩 DID I ACCOMPLISH MY FINANCIAL GOAL?

🧠 WHAT HAVE I LEARNED IN THE PAST 21 DAYS?

_____
_____
_____
_____

🪄 WHAT NEW SKILLS HAVE I ACQUIRED?

_____
_____
_____
_____

WHAT WERE THE BIGGEST CHALLENGES I HAD TO OVERCOME?

_____
_____
_____
_____

🏃 WHAT ARE MY NEXT STEPS?

_____
_____
_____
_____

Month of:

SUN	MON	TUES	WED	THU	FRI	SAT

Important Dates

My Financial Goal

⚑ WHAT IS MY FINANCIAL GOAL?

⚏ WHY DO I WANT TO ACHIEVE THIS GOAL?

❓ HOW WILL I ACHIEVE MY GOAL?

✈ WHAT TOOLS WILL I USE TO ACCOMPLISH MY GOAL?

My Financial Strategies

🚩 MY FINANCIAL GOAL IS ....

_____

_____

💡 STRATEGY #1

📋 5 ACTION STEPS

#1 _____
#2 _____
#3 _____
#4 _____
#5 _____

💡 STRATEGY #2

📋 5 ACTION STEPS

#1 _____
#2 _____
#3 _____
#4 _____
#5 _____

💡 STRATEGY #3

📋 5 ACTION STEPS

#1 _____
#2 _____
#3 _____
#4 _____
#5 _____

Reflection

🚩 DID I ACCOMPLISH MY FINANCIAL GOAL?

⚙️ WHAT HAVE I LEARNED IN THE PAST 21 DAYS?

_____
_____
_____
_____

🪄 WHAT NEW SKILLS HAVE I ACQUIRED?

_____
_____
_____
_____

🏔️ WHAT WERE THE BIGGEST CHALLENGES I HAD TO OVERCOME?

_____
_____
_____
_____

🏃 WHAT ARE MY NEXT STEPS?

_____
_____
_____
_____

Month of:

SUN	MON	TUES	WED	THU	FRI	SAT

Important Dates

_____   _____
_____   _____
_____   _____
_____   _____
_____   _____
_____   _____
_____   _____
_____   _____
_____   _____
_____   _____

My Financial Goal

🚩 WHAT IS MY FINANCIAL GOAL?

💡 WHY DO I WANT TO ACHIEVE THIS GOAL?

❓ HOW WILL I ACHIEVE MY GOAL?

WHAT TOOLS WILL I USE TO ACCOMPLISH MY GOAL?

My Financial Strategies

🚩 MY FINANCIAL GOAL IS ....

_____

_____

💡 **STRATEGY #1**

📋 **5 ACTION STEPS**

#1 _____
#2 _____
#3 _____
#4 _____
#5 _____

💡 **STRATEGY #2**

📋 **5 ACTION STEPS**

#1 _____
#2 _____
#3 _____
#4 _____
#5 _____

💡 **STRATEGY #3**

📋 **5 ACTION STEPS**

#1 _____
#2 _____
#3 _____
#4 _____
#5 _____

Reflection

 DID I ACCOMPLISH MY FINANCIAL GOAL?

WHAT HAVE I LEARNED IN THE PAST 21 DAYS?

_____
_____
_____
_____

WHAT NEW SKILLS HAVE I ACQUIRED?

_____
_____
_____
_____
_____

WHAT WERE THE BIGGEST CHALLENGES I HAD TO OVERCOME?

_____
_____
_____
_____

WHAT ARE MY NEXT STEPS?

_____
_____
_____
_____

Month of:

SUN	MON	TUES	WED	THU	FRI	SAT

Important Dates

_____ _____
_____ _____
_____ _____
_____ _____
_____ _____
_____ _____
_____ _____
_____ _____

My Financial Goal

🏳 WHAT IS MY FINANCIAL GOAL?

⬜

💡 WHY DO I WANT TO ACHIEVE THIS GOAL?

⬜

❓ HOW WILL I ACHIEVE MY GOAL?

⬜

📨 WHAT TOOLS WILL I USE TO ACCOMPLISH MY GOAL?

⬜

My Financial Strategies

🚩 MY FINANCIAL GOAL IS ....

_____

_____

💡 STRATEGY #1		📋 5 ACTION STEPS
		#1 _____
		#2 _____
		#3 _____
		#4 _____
		#5 _____

💡 STRATEGY #2		📋 5 ACTION STEPS
		#1 _____
		#2 _____
		#3 _____
		#4 _____
		#5 _____

💡 STRATEGY #3		📋 5 ACTION STEPS
		#1 _____
		#2 _____
		#3 _____
		#4 _____
		#5 _____

Reflection

 DID I ACCOMPLISH MY FINANCIAL GOAL?

✔ ✖

🧠 WHAT HAVE I LEARNED IN THE PAST 21 DAYS?

_____
_____
_____
_____

🪄 WHAT NEW SKILLS HAVE I ACQUIRED?

_____
_____
_____
_____

⛰ WHAT WERE THE BIGGEST CHALLENGES I HAD TO OVERCOME?

_____
_____
_____
_____

🏃 WHAT ARE MY NEXT STEPS?

_____
_____
_____
_____

Month of:

SUN	MON	TUES	WED	THU	FRI	SAT

Important Dates

My Financial Goal

🚩 WHAT IS MY FINANCIAL GOAL?

⬛ WHY DO I WANT TO ACHIEVE THIS GOAL?

❓ HOW WILL I ACHIEVE MY GOAL?

✈ WHAT TOOLS WILL I USE TO ACCOMPLISH MY GOAL?

My Financial Strategies

🚩 MY FINANCIAL GOAL IS ....

_____

_____

_____

💡 STRATEGY #1		📋 5 ACTION STEPS
		#1 _____
		#2 _____
		#3 _____
		#4 _____
		#5 _____

💡 STRATEGY #2		📋 5 ACTION STEPS
		#1 _____
		#2 _____
		#3 _____
		#4 _____
		#5 _____

💡 STRATEGY #3		📋 5 ACTION STEPS
		#1 _____
		#2 _____
		#3 _____
		#4 _____
		#5 _____

Reflection

 DID I ACCOMPLISH MY FINANCIAL GOAL?

✔   ✖

WHAT HAVE I LEARNED IN THE PAST 21 DAYS?

_____
_____
_____
_____

WHAT NEW SKILLS HAVE I ACQUIRED?

_____
_____
_____
_____
_____

WHAT WERE THE BIGGEST CHALLENGES I HAD TO OVERCOME?

_____
_____
_____
_____
_____

WHAT ARE MY NEXT STEPS?

_____
_____
_____
_____
_____

Journal

Connect With Tesha at
Smart Money Sisters

We help women master the money thing!
We show you how to make, manage, and multiply money.

WWW.SMARTMONEYSISTERS.COM

@TheSmartMoneySisters

@SmartMoneySisters

@SmartMoneySisters

@SmartMoneySisters

Tesha D. Colston

Tesha D. Colston is an Christian author, speaker, life coach and financial educator with over 15 years of experience in ministry. Known for her compassionate and empowering approach, Tesha has dedicated her life to inspiring and equipping women to achieve personal and financial growth through faith. She is a four-time Amazon Best-Selling author and a sought-after speaker who has been seen in various media outlets. Her life journey, filled with personal triumphs and unwavering faith, equips her to impact women with unique messages of hope, compassion, and simplicity, providing them with the necessary tools for meaningful and lasting change.

Connect

@TeshaDColston   @TeshaDColston   @TeshaDColston   @TeshaDColston

WWW.TESHADCOLSTON.COM

www.ingramcontent.com/pod-product-compliance
Lightning Source LLC
Chambersburg PA
CBHW071828210526